# CHINESE PICTURES

## CHINA THROUGH THE EYES OF
### ISABELLA BIRD

With a Foreword by
Graham Earnshaw

Chinese Pictures
by Isabella Bird
With a foreword by Graham Earnshaw

ISBN-978-988-8552-44-3

© 2019 Earnshaw Books

HISTORY / Asia / China

EB118

All rights reserved. No part of this book may be reproduced in material form, by any means, whether graphic, electronic, mechanical or other, including photocopying or information storage, in whole or in part. May not be used to prepare other publications without written permission from the publisher except in the case of brief quotations embodied in critical articles or reviews. For information contact info@earnshawbooks.com

Published by Earnshaw Books Ltd. (Hong Kong)

# FOREWORD

## Graham Earnshaw

IN THE LATE 1890s, Isabella L. Bird was renowned throughout the English-speaking world and beyond as one of the greatest travelers, and probably the pre-eminent travel writer, of the day. But by then, she was also an avid photographer, a pursuit she took up in 1894 at the age of sixty-three. It is this element of her life that is glimpsed though the pages of this book.

*Chinese Pictures* was the last book published during her lifetime and it contains sixty-one photographs with a commentary beside each one, written by someone other than Isabella, but clearly based upon comments made by her.

The subjects of the photographs included reflect, inevitably, Isabella's life while in China which was mostly spent in travel. She presents many images of modes of transportation, of city gates and of paths and waterways, because she was always on the move. There are some images of sights and people she saw along the way, but she was never long enough anywhere to get behind the screen. And anyway, life as a foreigner in China in those days was one of incredible isolation and separation, both imposed and self-created.

Isabella Bird was born in Yorkshire in northern England in 1831, the daughter of a clergyman. She was small in stature, and suffered from various health problems as a child, leading to an operation at the age of nineteen to remove a tumor from her spine. After the operation, she suffered from insomnia and depression, and her doctor recommended that she travel, so in 1854 aged twenty-three, she went to North America and stayed there for several months. On her return, she wrote her first book about her experiences, *The Englishwoman in America*.

She continued to travel and to write, but it was a visit to the Hawaiian islands in 1872 in her early forties that changed her life. She was on a ship from San Francisco heading for New Zealand, but decided to get off in Hawaii, and spent six months there, visiting all the main islands, riding horses up and down the volcanoes and writing about an island chain and a culture which at that time was still very much like the one encountered by Captain James Cook when he had visited a century before. Her book, *Six Months in the Sandwich Islands, was published in 1875*. She then spent time in the west of the United States, including several months snowed into a log cabin in the Rocky Mountains, an adventure told in her book *A Lady's Life in the Rocky Mountains*, published in 1879.

She sailed across the Pacific again to Japan and traveled for several months through that country with an interpreter, reaching the northern part of Hokkaido where she stayed with the Ainu tribes, the original inhabitants of the Japan islands. Her book on this experience, *Unbeaten Tracks in Japan*, was published in 1880. She then went to Hong Kong, Canton, Saigon, Singapore and the Malay Peninsula, and of course wrote another book on that trip.

On her return to England, she found herself to be famous, but her sister died of typhoid soon after her return and Isabella married the doctor who had taken care of her, Dr. John Bishop, in 1881. Inconsiderately, he also died only five years later, and Isabella resumed her travels. In 1888, she was in India, and traveled to Kashmir and on into the border lands of western Tibet. And from 1894 to 1898 she traveled through Korea, Japan and China, and was almost killed in an anti-foreigner riot in the city of Chengdu, in Sichuan province. That trip resulted in the book *The Yangtze*

*Valley and Beyond*, published in response to the intense interest in China that resulted from the Boxer uprising in 1900, the siege of the Legation Quarter in Peking and the murder of many missionaries across the country. The photographs in this collection were all taken during that trip.

In 1902, with the Boxer troubles over, she very much wanted to make another trip to China, but medical problems meant she had to lower her sights and went to Morocco instead. It was her last trip. On her return, she was bedridden until she died two years later in 1904, in Edinburgh.

A late starter to the world of photography, Isabella embraced the technology enthusiastically. She attended an advanced photography course at the Regent Street Polytechnic in 1894, and had two cameras with her when she set off on that last long trip through East Asia. At the time, the tripod, photographic equipment, plates and paraphernalia involved were extremely cumbersome, but Miss Bird would have had coolies and helpers to do the carrying while she went ahead scouting for photographable scenes, usually seated on a covered chair held aloft by two men carrying poles, but sometimes walking or riding a horse. She took pictures constantly, especially in China.

In her book *The Yangtze Valley and Beyond*, she describes her visit to Shanghai's Chinese city, made against the advice of virtually all the foreigners living there.

> I absolutely failed to get an escort until Mr. Fox, of H.M's Consular Service, kindly offered to accompany me. I did not take back small-pox or any other malady, I was not rudely jostled by dirty coolies, nor was I hurt or knocked down by wheelbarrows. The slush and the smells were there, but the slush was not fouler nor the smells more abominable than in other big Chinese cities that I have walked through; and as a foreign woman is an everyday sight in the near neighborhood, the people minded their own business and not mine, and I

was even able to photograph without being overborne by the curious.

There are references in her other writings to all sorts of scenes being photographed. In *Yangtze Valley*, she recounts a story of photographing members of the Chinese Viceroy's military guard at a foreign-operated hospital in front of a large audience of Chinese onlookers who used the opportunity to make fun of the soldiers in light of the recent defeat of the Qing dynasty forces in Korea in the face of well-equipped and well-trained Japanese forces.

> On one occasion when I was photographing four soldiers of the Viceroy's guard in the hospital grounds the hilarity burst all bounds, and the distempered mass yelled with enjoyment. When I photographed the backs of the soldiers they shouted, "She pictures their backs because they ran away from the "wojen" (dwarfs); and when Dr. Main displayed their brawny legs, they nearly danced with the fun of it, yelling, "Those are the legs they ran away on." Not that the Viceroy's guard had encountered the Japanese, but these people were near enough to Shanghai to have heard of the figure the Chinese troops had cut.

She spent much time in and around Shanghai, and traveled on one occasion south to the city of Shaoxing, where she was hosted by a missionary, the Reverend W.G. Walshe. While there, she once more demonstrated the complete fearlessness which was a fundamental part of her character.

"Her absolute unconsciousness of fear was a remarkable characteristic," Walshe later wrote; "and even in remote places, where large crowds assembled to witness her photographic performances, she never seemed in the least to realise the possibility of danger. Had she done so, she would have missed a great deal of what she saw and learned. On more than one occasion I was conscious of a feeling of nervousness, though I flattered myself that I knew something of the character of the people among whom I lived; but even in the face of the largest and noisiest crowds, Mrs Bishop proceeded with her photography and observations as calmly as if she were inspecting some of the Chinese exhibitions in the British Museum."

From Shanghai, she travelled up the Yangtze River by ship to Hankow, part of today's Wuhan, and was in constant need of space and facilities to develop photographic images. She sailed on west from Hankow on an American-built, stern-wheel steamer, the *Chang-wo*, heading for the Yangtze Gorges.

> The captain was kind and genial. He let me tone unlimited photographic prints in the saloon, ignoring the dishes and buckets involved in the process, and the engineer provided an unlimited supply of condensed water, free both from Yangtze mud and from the alum used to precipitate it. But he had a unique affluence of bad language, which neither the presence of clergy nor women sufficed to check, and which was brought out with slow, thrilling, and emphatically damnatory deliberation on the many occasions on which we ran on shoals. I had abundant occupation in writing, printing and toning photographs, learning a little from Mr. Endacott of the region for which I was finally bound, taking walks below past the Chinese cabins, where the inmates were reclining in the bliss of opium.

She traversed the gorges with their tricky rapids and the long stretches of the Yangtze beyond in small Chinese boats, taking and developing photographs the whole way, "all the blankets and waterproofs in the boat being requisitioned for the creation of a "dark room", as she put it.

She landed at Wanhsien, today's Wanzhou, a place with only one foreign missionary mission at the time and no more than a handful of foreigners.

> So it came about that for several days I was able actually to walk about and to photograph with no worse trouble than the curiosity of the people in masculine crowds of a thousand or more. Four months before I was told that this would have been impossible. My camera would have been smashed, my open chair would have produced a riot, and I should have been stoned or severely beaten.

From there, she headed directly west, away from the river across the Szechuan basin towards Chengdu, the capital of the province, with her entourage of coolies.

When they had fed and smoked, the men shouldered their burdens, and trudged on till about sunset, stopping, as in the morning, for smokes and drinks, I walking and photographing as it suited me. Sometimes we put up at a wayside inn, without even the privacy of a yard; this was in very small places, where the curiosity was not so overwhelming.

In Sichuan, she constantly came up against anti-foreign sentiment, including in the town of Jialing:

> The people are not what would be called hostile, yet they curse Mr. James, the missionary, in the streets, and believe that all the five are "child-eaters," and that the comeliness of the ladies is preserved by the use of children's brains! This scandalous accusation is current everywhere in SZE CHUAN. Even at quiet Chia-ling Fu, when two beggar boys were brought into the compound to be photographed, the report spread like wildfire through the city that they had been taken in for the purpose of

being fatted for eating!

Then beyond Chengdu, she headed up into the mountains to the west that form the beginning of the Tibetan plateau. She had been on the southwest portion of Tibet a few years earlier, and clearly loved the high altitudes in spite of the hardships and dangers of travel and the extremes of weather.

> The journey from first to last was magnificent, but the wind, which I found such a merciless foe in Central Asia, rose at the same hour, 9 a.m., and blew half a gale till near sunset, reaching its maximum of force at 2 p.m., making photography impossible, several times nearly overturning the chair and its bearers.

Her best description of photography in China is of developing negatives and prints while sailing up or down the Yangtze, in an age when darkness was truly dark:

> Above all, there were photographic negatives to develop and print, and prints to tone, and the difficulties enhanced the zest of these processes and made me think, with a feeling of complacent superiority, of the amateurs who need "dark rooms", sinks, water "laid on", tables and other luxuries. Night supplied me with a dark room; the majestic Yangtze was "laid on"; a box served for a table; all else can be dispensed with. I lined my "stall" with muslin curtains and newspapers, and finding that the light of the opium lamps still came in through the chinks, I tacked up my blankets and slept in my clothes and fur coat. With "water water everywhere", water was the great difficulty. The Yangtze holds any amount of fine mud in

suspension, which for drinking purposes is usually precipitated with alum, and unless filtered, deposits a fine, even veil on the negative. I had only a pocket filter, which produced about three quarts of water a day, of which Be-dien [her servant] invariably abstracted some for making tea, leaving me with only enough for a final wash, not always quite effectual, as the critic will see from some of the illustrations. I found that the most successful method of washing out "hypo" was to lean out over the gunwale and hold the negative in the wash of the Great River, rapid even at the mooring place, and give it some final washes in the filtered water…. Printing was a great difficulty, and I only overcame it by hanging the printing-frames over the side. When all these rough arrangements were successful, each print was a joy and a triumph, nor was there any disgrace in failure.

A few brief notes on the images themselves.

The first four photographs in the book and several other images of gates and walls were taken by her in the capital Peking in 1898, before the massive ruction of the Boxer Rebellion and its aftermath.

The coolie-carried palanquin (page 23) is of interest because Isabella would have traveled often in just such a contraption. The caption doesn't say so, but the chances are this was a palanquin that she herself used. Similarly, the photograph of a small houseboat on the Yangtze River (page 34), is not identified as one in which she travelled, but it probably was.

The image of coolies carrying oil and wine (page 28) is of interest to me personally, in that I saw men using the same stick approach to carrying heavy loads in the mountains of Sichuan in 2007, more than a hundred years after she took these images. Also the woven shoes on the dying coolie (page 64) were still being worn in the Sichuan countryside in the early 21$^{st}$ century, by some older men.

# CHINESE PICTURES

Notes on Photographs

Made in China

by
MRS. J. F. BISHOP
F.R.G.S., etc.

# INTRODUCTION

THIS LITTLE BOOK is the outcome of talks with Mrs. Bishop over some of the photographs which were taken by her in one or other of her journeys into and across China. Some of the photographs have already appeared in her published works, "The Yangtze Valley and Beyond" and "Korea and Her Neighbourhood" (2 vols., Murray). The notes were, in substance, dictated by Mrs. Bishop. It is hoped they contain some real information on the people, their surroundings, and habits which, though slight in form, may be helpful to a better understanding of a very difficult problem.

According to our newspaper press to-day, the Chinese are simply cruel barbarians. According to Mrs. Bishop, when you know them they are a likeable people—and she has formed this opinion in spite of the fact that, in their deeply-rooted hatred of the foreigners, they twice attacked her with violence. A real understanding of the people is for us, with our different modes of thought, most difficult to arrive at; but we shall not advance towards it by accepting all the evil reports and shutting our ears to the good ones. That the problem of China is, and will for some time continue to be, the most interesting question to the rest of the world is certain. The future of its people is all unknown, but there are in it possibilities which make it a terror to all other nations.

ISABELLA BIRD

# CONTENTS

| | |
|---|---|
| The Private Entrance to the Imperial Palace, Peking | 8 |
| The Entrance to the British Legation | 10 |
| Entrance to the College of the Student Interpreters | 12 |
| The State Carriage of the British Legation | 14 |
| The Great Imperial Stone Road From Peking to Chengtu, The Capital of Sze Chuan | 16 |
| A Mule Cart | 18 |
| A Manchurian Family Travelling | 20 |
| Carriage by Bearers | 22 |
| A Traveller Arriving at An Inn in Manchuria | 24 |
| Carriage of Merchandise | 26 |
| The Mode of Carrying Oil and Wine | 28 |
| Wheelbarrow Traffic on the Chengtu Plain | 30 |
| The Wheelbarrow of North China | 32 |
| A Small Houseboat on the Yangtze Kiang | 34 |
| A Foot Boat Found in Central China | 36 |
| Hsin Tan Rapid on the Yangtze River | 38 |
| A Boat on the Min River, Used for Running the Rapids | 40 |

| | |
|---|---|
| Part of a Fringe of Junks or River Boats at Wan Hsien | 42 |
| The Bridge of Ten Thousand Ages, Foochow | 44 |
| A Bridge at Wan Hsien of the Single Arch Type | 46 |
| The Bridge of Mien Chuh Sze Chuan | 48 |
| A Simple Country Bridge | 50 |
| A Dragon Bridge | 52 |
| The Zig-zag Bridge of Shanghai | 54 |
| The Garden of the Guild of Benevolence, Chung King | 56 |
| A Burial Charity | 58 |
| A Baby Tower, Foochow | 60 |
| Bottle Seller and Hospital Patient | 62 |
| The Dying Coolie | 64 |
| The Mode of Sepulchre throughout Southern China | 66 |
| Coffins Kept Above Ground | 68 |
| The Temple of the God of Literature at Mukden | 70 |
| The Temple of the Fox, Mukden | 72 |
| Wayside Shrines | 74 |
| The Ficus Religiosa | 76 |
| The Altar of Heaven | 78 |
| The Tablet of Confucius | 80 |
| A Porcelain-fronted Temple on the Yangtze | 82 |
| Child Eating Rice with Chopsticks | 84 |

# CHINESE PICTURES

| | |
|---|---|
| Fort on the Peking Wall | 86 |
| Another Fort on the Wall of Peking | 88 |
| Colossal Astronomical Instruments on the Peking Wall | 90 |
| Chien Mun Gate | 92 |
| The Gate of Victory, Mukden | 94 |
| The West Gate of Kialing Fu | 96 |
| The West Gate of Hangchow | 98 |
| The Gate of a Forbidden City | 100 |
| Silk Reeling | 102 |
| A Typical Entrance to a House | 104 |
| The Guest Hall in a Chinese House, Wan Hsien, Sze Chuan | 106 |
| A Chinese Village | 108 |
| A Farmhouse in the Hakka Country, Southern China | 110 |
| A Market Place or Market Street in Sze Chuan | 112 |
| The Cobbler | 114 |
| Carrying Liquid Manure to the Fields | 116 |
| The Marriage Chair | 118 |
| Mode of Carrying Cash and Babies | 120 |
| A Pai-fang, or Widow's Arch | 122 |
| Two Soldiers of Sze Chuan | 124 |
| Opium Culture Encroaching on the Rice Lands, Sze Chuan | 126 |

## THE PRIVATE ENTRANCE TO THE IMPERIAL PALACE. PEKING.

A subject of considerable interest, owing to the mystery surrounding the members of the Imperial Family. The photograph was taken from the wall of the Purple or Forbidden City, in which only the Imperial Family and their entourage have the right to dwell. The building in the centre, which is roofed with yellow tiles, is supposed to be the residence of the Emperor, but where he does actually reside remains a mystery. The entrance to the Palace is through the arches in the building on the left.

THE PRIVATE ENTRANCE TO THE IMPERIAL PALACE. PEKING.

## THE ENTRANCE TO THE BRITISH LEGATION.

The Legation is a fine old palace, which formerly belonged to a member of the Imperial Family. The photograph shows the entrance to the first courtyard. The Legation compound is very extensive, and contains several courtyards with buildings round each. It is very highly decorated, the designs shown in this picture being elaborately wrought in lacquered work of gold and colours. This is the building recently attacked by the Chinese in their attempt to destroy all foreigners, including the members of the various European Legations who took refuge with Sir Claude Macdonald.

CHINESE PICTURES

THE ENTRANCE TO THE BRITISH LEGATION.

## ENTRANCE TO THE COLLEGE OF THE STUDENT INTERPRETERS.

Student interpreters are young Englishmen who enter the College to prepare themselves for the Consular Service. At eighteen they have to pass Their entrance examination. They receive given posts in connection with one of the various Chinese Consulates. All our Chinese Consuls are drawn from this College. It stands within the grounds of the Legation, which is the building shown on the right of the picture.

ENTRANCE TO THE COLLEGE OF THE STUDENT INTERPRETERS.

## THE STATE CARRIAGE OF THE BRITISH LEGATION.

There are practically no carriage roads in China, so that there is virtually no carriage traffic. This rough, springless cart is the only carriage drawn by animals at the disposal of the Legation.

THE STATE CARRIAGE OF THE BRITISH LEGATION.

# THE GREAT IMPERIAL STONE ROAD FROM PEKING TO CHENGTU, THE CAPITAL OF SZE CHUAN.

Made more than a thousand years ago, it must have been a gigantic work at the time of its construction. It was paved throughout with rough stone flags for about eight feet, or about half its width, and planted with cedars. It is now very much out of repair, as are most things in China, the flags disappearing now and again for long distances; but it is still the object of much official attention, and every year certain magistrates inspect it and count the cedars, every one of which is sealed with the Imperial seal. Many of the trees have died, but many still survive and are grand objects by the roadside.

# CHINESE PICTURES

THE GREAT IMPERIAL STONE ROAD FROM PEKING TO CHENGTU, THE CAPITAL OF SZE CHUAN.

## A MULE CART.

A TYPICAL mode of conveyance in Manchuria, the Northern Province. The arrangement for carrying luggage is seen at the back of the cart. It is very similar to the Legation state carriage in construction, being entirely without springs. It is only possible to use such a conveyance in such a roadless country, with any security from broken bones, by adopting the precaution to pad the whole of the interior, bottom, top, and sides with thick mattresses. In the course of a journey of three miles only, Mrs. Bishop had the misfortune to be thrown into the top of the cart in an upset with such violence that her arm was broken and her head severely cut. In her case, unfortunately, the top of the cart was not padded.

CHINESE PICTURES

A MULE CART.

## A MANCHURIAN FAMILY TRAVELLING.

Although so risky to life and limb, the mule cart is the more fashionable mode of moving from place to place in Manchuria. The poorer people ride on asses, with their belongings slung about in the manner shown in the picture.

# CHINESE PICTURES

## A MANCHURIAN FAMILY TRAVELLING.

## CARRIAGE BY BEARERS.

Out in the country there are practically no roads, as we understand roads. It is necessary to cultivate every inch of available ground, and the farmer begrudges anything taken from the fields for the paths, which are but a foot or two wide. It is easy to understand that, under such conditions, the almost universal mode of passenger transit is by chairs and bearers. The narrowness of the paths is a source of trouble. When two parties of bearers approach each other, there is much shouting to induce one or other to return and make way; but when both come on, one has to get off, or be pushed off, into the swamp by the sides. When one is a foreigner his portion is invariably the swamp.

The bearers are patient, much-enduring people, who do their work thoroughly and without complaining, in the face of mud, and rain, and difficult roads. They will carry a traveller from twenty to twenty-five miles a day. When a lady occupies the chair the curtains are rigidly closed. It would be at the risk of her life to travel in an open chair. There is much etiquette connected with the getting in and out of chairs, which wise travellers never neglect. The photograph is of a lady's chair.

CHINESE PICTURES

CARRIAGE BY BEARERS.

# A TRAVELLER ARRIVING AT AN INN IN MANCHURIA.

There are various ways of carrying a traveller's baggage. Sometimes it is slung in the centre of bars and carried as the traveller's own chair is carried. More often a package is slung at each end of a bar, which is placed across the shoulders of a coolie. Constant change of shoulder is necessary, and the stopping to make this change becomes a serious matter in a journey of any length. It is trying work, and the shoulders of the coolies generally show it by the callositis produced by the constant carrying of heavy burdens. The illustration shows Mrs. Bishop's baggage arriving after a day's journey.

A TRAVELLER ARRIVING AT AN INN
IN MANCHURIA.

## CARRIAGE OF MERCHANDISE.

It will be seen that two coolies, by means of these bars, can carry a great weight—as much as two hundred pounds is carried between them—and they will cover with this weight twenty to twenty-five miles a day. Chair-carriers will, with the attendant luggage-carriers, cover as much as twenty-five miles, but their burdens are less heavy.

CARRIAGE OF MERCHANDISE.

## THE MODE OF CARRYING OIL AND WINE

In wicker baskets lined with oiled paper of extraordinary toughness, which is much used everywhere. The oil is obtained from various "oil seeds," the tough paper by macerating bamboo. Beneath the basket will be noticed a long cylinder. This is the coolie's purse, in which he carries his "cash," the small copper or brass coin of the country, which is of such small value that nine pounds weight of copper cash is only worth one English shilling.

THE MODE OF CARRYING OIL AND WINE.

## WHEELBARROW TRAFFIC ON THE CHENGTU PLAIN.

This Chengtu Plain, with its 2,500 square miles of country and 4,000,000 population, is perhaps the best cultivated and most fertile spot in the world. It owes its fertility to the work of two engineers, who, more than two thousand years ago (250 years B.C.), designed and carried out the most perfect system of irrigation. They were Li Ping, the father, and his son, and are familiarly known to-day as the first and second gentlemen of China. The land bears four crops in the year. With all this produce and population the traffic is enormous, and it is mainly carried on by means of wheelbarrows, which are so contrived, by placing the wheel in the centre and platforms at the side and behind it, as to enable one man to wheel five hundredweight with ease. The narrow roads of the plain are covered by an almost endless procession of these wheelbarrows, which are often preceded by one man pulling in addition to the man behind.

WHEELBARROW TRAFFIC ON THE CHENGTU PLAIN.

# THE WHEELBARROW OF NORTH CHINA.

This is another form of the same baggage-carrier which is in use all over the Empire. It is much larger than that in use on the Plain of Chengtu, but is constructed on the same principle; by means of it one man can wheel as much as half a ton. It is a vehicle well adapted to the narrow roads of the country.

THE WHEELBARROW OF NORTH CHINA.

## A SMALL HOUSEBOAT ON THE YANGTZE KIANG.

If China cannot boast of its roads, it may claim to be a country of waterways, rivers and canals forming the chief means of communication. The country being so large, travellers have to spend much time in going from place to place, and living accommodation has to be provided on the boats. It is very rough. The illustration gives a good specimen of a small boat which may be hired for a journey. The mat roof is placed over the open part at night. In the daytime this space is occupied by the rowers. In the night they roll themselves up in their wadded quilts and sleep there. In China there is no privacy, but much curiosity. No part of your boat, although you have hired it, Is sacred to you; the boatmen pass in and out of what you may regard as your cabin without consideration for you. Mrs. Bishop put up curtains around her cabin to shut out prying eyes, and as far as they could the people respected her evident desire to be alone.

CHINESE PICTURES

A SMALL HOUSEBOAT ON THE YANGTZE KIANG.

## A FOOT BOAT FOUND IN CENTRAL CHINA.

The oars are worked by the feet instead of the arms. The sides of this one are beautifully carved and lacquered, and protection from the sun and rain is provided by a roof of mats, the universal form of shelter and protection on the water.

A FOOT BOAT FOUND IN CENTRAL CHINA.

# HSIN TAN RAPID ON THE YANGTZE RIVER.

The rapids on the river give rise to a considerable amount of occupation for men called Trackers, whose occupation is the dragging of boats up-stream through the wild and dangerous waters of the rapids. These men live in huts on the river banks as close to the water's edge as possible. A group of their huts is to be seen on the left of the picture, and on the extreme left, almost too small to be visible, are four hundred trackers dragging up a boat. At the top and foot of every rapid on the Yangtze are to be found one or more Red Lifeboats, which are most efficiently and admirably manned and maintained at the cost of Benevolent Guilds—one of the many charitable guilds in the country — for the purpose of assisting the crews of boats which get into difficulties. Boats are frequently wrecked in their passage, and the Red Lifeboat has saved the lives of many foreigners in the accidents attendant upon their passage of the Rapids.

HSIN TAN RAPID ON THE YANGTZE RIVER.

## A BOAT ON THE MIN RIVER, USED FOR RUNNING THE RAPIDS.

The Min River, called also the Fu, is a western tributary of the Upper Yangtze, but a great river in itself. Of the boat's four sails the lowest is of bamboo, and is let down at night to protect the boatman and his family. The feature of the boat is its high prow, for protection against the rocks and rushing water.

A BOAT ON THE MIN RIVER, USED FOR RUNNING THE RAPIDS.

## PART OF A FRINGE OF JUNKS OR RIVER BOATS AT WAN HSIEN.

Illustrating the enormous traffic on the Yangtze. This fringe of boats, closely packed, extends for two miles along the river bank, and is an evidence of the great trade and prosperity of Wan Hsien.

PART OF A FRINGE OF JUNKS OR RIVER BOATS
AT WAN HSIEN.

# THE BRIDGE OF TEN THOUSAND AGES, FOOCHOW.

A country of waterways must be a country of bridges, but the beauty of the bridges in China is quite a surprise to the traveller. The straight bridge of the illustration given here is built upon enormously solid piers, which are often monoliths. The roadway is constructed of single blocks thirty feet long. The balustrade, as well as the roadway, is solid stone. This is the oldest form of bridge in the country, and the bridge in the picture is one of the oldest bridges.

CHINESE PICTURES

THE BRIDGE OF TEN THOUSAND AGES,
FOOCHOW.

## A BRIDGE AT WAN HSIEN OF THE SINGLE ARCH TYPE.

One enters almost every town or village, when travelling by water, under a bridge of one arch, which may be anything from fifteen to thirty feet high and of a most graceful form. These bridges are constructed of blocks of granite cut to the curve of the bridge, and a flight of steps leads to the crown of the arch. In the illustration the steps are clearly shown leading to the house at the top. A most graceful and beautiful bridge.

A BRIDGE AT WAN HSIEN OF THE
SINGLE ARCH TYPE.

## THE BRIDGE OF MIEN CHUH SZE CHUAN.

When a rich man or a company of rich men wish to benefit their province, it is quite a common thing for them to let their generosity take the form of the building of a bridge. This bridge was so built. It is a most beautiful structure, both in form and colour. The roof is of green tiles, the inside being lined with crimson lacquer, deeply incised in gold with the names of the donors.

THE BRIDGE OF MIEN CHUH SZE CHUAN.

## A SIMPLE COUNTRY BRIDGE.

The kind of bridge found on a secondary road in Sze Chuan, constructed of wood roofed in with tiles, after the manner of Switzerland, to protect it from the weather.

# CHINESE PICTURES

**A SIMPLE COUNTRY BRIDGE.**

## A DRAGON BRIDGE.

Quite a common form of stone bridge, in which every pier is surmounted by a dragon, the national emblem.

A DRAGON BRIDGE.

# THE ZIG-ZAG BRIDGE OF SHANGHAI.

Its name indicates its peculiar character. It makes nine zig-zags across the water to the most celebrated tea house in Shanghai, and, perhaps, the most fashionable tea house in China. It is the resort of mandarins and people of the upper classes. Women are never seen at the tea houses. They are patronised by men only. Women, indeed, are very little seen in public at all. The absence of the female element is a marked feature in Chinese life.

THE ZIG-ZAG BRIDGE OF SHANGHAI.

## THE GARDEN OF THE GUILD OF BENEVOLENCE, CHUNG KING.

China is the country of guilds. All workmen and traders have their guilds. To this rule there are but two exceptions — the water-carriers and the trackers (men who drag the boats up the rapids); these alone have no trade organisation. These guilds, or trade unions, are as complete and as effective for good or harm as anything we know in this country. They watch most jealously the interests of their craft. But the guild enters into the life of the people at every' turn. The charities of the Empire, which are numerous, are conducted by guilds. There is, perhaps, little personal charity and benevolence; it is safer to leave these to the guilds. But there is scarcely a town of any size that has not its Guild of Benevolence. Soup kitchens, clothing for the living, coffins and burial for the dead, hospitals, free dispensaries, orphan and foundling homes, life-boats, and many other charities are the outcome of these Guilds of Beneveolence.

THE GARDEN OF THE GUILD OF BENEVOLENCE,
CHUNG KING.

## A BURIAL CHARITY.

A cemetery, with temple attached, for the burial, with all sacred rites, of strangers who may have died friendless. To a Chinaman the most important event in his history is his burial. We can have no idea of what decent burial means to him. He is thinking of it and arranging for it all his life, and it is not to be wondered at that so large a part of the operation of Chinese charity should connect itself with funerals. To be suitably buried is the great hope and aim of every Chinaman.

This Cemetery, with its funeral rites, is one of the operations of a Guild of Benevolence.

A BURIAL CHARITY.

## A BABY TOWER, FOOCHOW.

When a baby dies, and the parents are too poor to give it a decent burial, they drop its poor little body into one of the openings in this tower. A Guild of Benevolence charges itself with the task of clearing out the tower every two or three days, burying the bodies with all religious rites and ceremony.

CHINESE PICTURES

A BABY TOWER, FOOCHOW.

## BOTTLE SELLER AND HOSPITAL PATIENT.

The hospitals of England and China have evidently many things in common. Inside the compound of the English Presbyterian Medical Mission of Swatow, the patients buy their bottles of the vendor as if they were patients of Guy's or St. Bartholomew's. A similar incident is to be witnessed in Smithfield any day of the week. It may be mentioned that the hospital of this particular Medical Mission is nearly the largest in the East. In times of stress it accommodates four hundred patients, and in the proportion of its cures is one of the most successful in the world.

BOTTLE SELLER AND HOSPITAL PATIENT.

# THE DYING COOLIE.

Perhaps because benevolence and charity are the objects of guilds, there is very little of the personal element in either. Personal kindliness and care for the sick and dying do not characterise the people of China. If a man is sick to death he is of no more use, and why should time and care be wasted on him? This coolie in the picture was one of Mrs. Bishop's carriers, who fell sick by the way, and though he had been a companion of the other men for many days, they had no care for him when he fell sick, and Mrs. Bishop was laughed at for taking the trouble to wet a handkerchief to lay on the feverish forehead of a man who was of "no more use."

**THE DYING COOLIE.**

## THE MODE OF SEPULCHRE THROUGHOUT SOUTHERN CHINA.

A horseshoe-shaped excavation is made in a hillside facing south, the whole construction being faced with stone. There is in this mode of arranging graves a similarity to that adopted by the Etruscans.

CHINESE PICTURES

THE MODE OF SEPULCHRE THROUGHOUT SOUTHERN CHINA.

## COFFINS KEPT ABOVE GROUND.

So careful is the Chinaman about his burial, that the date and place of a funeral is not fixed until the geomancers have decided as to both. Sometimes the coffins with their inmates remain above ground for months, and even years, waiting for the professional decision as to a favourable day. In such cases, where the friends are able, every care is taken of them, incense being daily burned before them. It was no uncommon thing for Mrs. Bishop, on her journey in Sze Chuan, to have to sleep in a room where a coffin was stored, waiting the day of its interment, incense burning and other religious rites being daily performed in front of it. To prevent mischief owing to the retention of bodies above ground for so long a time, the coffins are built of very thick wood, the bodies are placed in lime, the joints of the coffin are cemented, and the whole covered with varnish.

COFFINS KEPT ABOVE GROUND.

# THE GOD OF LITERATURE AT MUKDEN.

Mukden is the capital of Manchuria, the Northern Province. In every province of the Empire the God of Literature stands highest in the Chinese Pantheon, and it is interesting to note that the God of War stands low, though in China, as in other countries, we know women are devoted to his worship. In no country of the world does literature stand in such high estimation; by means of it the poorest man may climb to the highest post in the Empire. Nothing so helps a man to a career as a knowledge of the literature of his country. Reverence for it has become a superstition, and societies exist for collecting waste paper and saving any writing from indignity by burning it in furnaces erected for the purpose in every town.

THE GOD OF LITERATURE AT MUKDEN.

# THE TEMPLE OF THE FOX, MUKDEN.

Another temple at Mukden, greatly frequented by mandarins. A group of them is seated in the centre. The temple is situated close to the city wall, which is shown in process of decay, the descending roots of the trees stripping off its facing, which lies and will continue to lie on the ground. It is an admirable illustration of the way things are allowed to go to ruin in China. The Chinese will undertake new works; they seldom repair old ones, and an aspect of decay is consequently frequently visible.

THE TEMPLE OF THE FOX, MUKDEN.

## WAYSIDE SHRINES.

Found all over the country, and commonly known as "Joss Houses." There is an idol in each of them. They are of interest as presenting a similar feature to the shrine and wayside crucifixes found all over Catholic countries in Europe.

# CHINESE PICTURES

## A WAYSIDE SHRINE.

## THE FICUS RELIGIOSA.

A KIND of banyan tree found in every village of the South and South Central Provinces of China. Its foliage covers an enormous extent of ground. The tree itself is an object of worship, and an altar for the burning of incense is always found beneath it.

THE FICUS RELIGIOSA.

## THE ALTAR OF HEAVEN.

A fine picture of an open-air altar Outside Foochow City.

THE ALTAR OF HEAVEN.

## THE TABLET OF CONFUCIUS.

Wherever there is a magistrate there is a temple to Confucius, in which the magistrates do homage in memory of the Great Teacher. The tablet is inscribed with a number of his most important sayings having a bearing on the administration of justice. This great man has by his teaching dominated the laws, the teaching, the literature, and the whole social life of nearly half the human race for the last two thousand years. These shrines are absolutely taboo to the foreigner, a fact which was learned by the traveller only after she had entered it and, finding it absolutely empty, had made her photograph.

THE TABLET OF CONFUCIUS.

## A PORCELAIN-FRONTED TEMPLE ON THE YANGTZE.

The manufacture of porcelain has for centuries made China celebrated. It may be of interest to refer to the fact that we owe the existence of our Worcester porcelain works to the Attempt made by a chemist to produce Porcelain in England similar to the Chinese. A great many temples in the Empire province of Sze Chuan have their fronts and roofs of this porcelain. They are most gorgeous in colour, and have the appearance of being jewelled.

A PORCELAIN-FRONTED TEMPLE
ON THE YANGTZE.

# CHILD EATING RICE WITH CHOPSTICKS.

The Chinese eat an enormous number of things which the Westerner turns from, or which he doesn't know of. As a rule the Chinese are good cooks, and the food is wholesome, steaming being the favourite method. Rice is the staff of life to the masses, who eat it mixed with fried cabbage or some other flavouring ingredient. It is seldom eaten alone. So common and universal is rice eating that, while in French the equivalent of "How do you do?" is "How do you carry yourself?" and in Italian "How do you stay?" in Chinese the equivalent is "Have you eaten rice?"

CHILD EATING RICE WITH CHOPSTICKS.

## FORT ON THE PEKING WALL.

City walls are a great feature of the country. The illustration is of a fort on one of the angles of the wall of Peking, the interest of it lying in the fact that the guns showing in the embrasures are dummies, being simply painted wood. Probably the cost of real guns went into the pockets of some official entrusted with providing the armament of the fort.

FORT ON THE PEKING WALL.

## ANOTHER FORT ON THE WALL OF PEKING.

This fort is filled with carronades, old guns still kept there, though absolutely useless, being honeycombed with disuse and rust.

ANOTHER FORT ON THE WALL OF PEKING.

## COLOSSAL ASTRONOMICAL INSTRUMENTS ON THE PEKING WALL.

Many hundred years old, but as bronze castings they are reckoned to be amongst the finest in the world. And as astronomical instruments their results differ very little from those obtained by astronomers from appliances of the most modern construction.

COLOSSAL ASTRONOMICAL INSTRUMENTS
ON THE PEKING WALL.

## CHIEN MUN GATE.

Perhaps the most interesting and picturesque feature of the country is its city gates. There is a great family Likeness between them, the usual fort-like building surmounting the wall where it is pierced by the gate. It is not a fort, however. In it are kept the gongs and other musical instruments by means of which are announced the rising and the setting of the sun. This is the gate which was blown up by the Japanese in their recent attack on and entry into the city. It is the largest and most important gate in Peking.

CHINESE PICTURES

**CHIEN MUN GATE.**

# THE GATE OF VICTORY, MUKDEN.

Mukden, the capital of Manchuria, is officially the second city of the Empire. In it are duplicated all the official boards, save one, that exist in Peking, the capital of the Empire. Thus Mukden possesses its Board of Rites and Ceremonies, of Punishments, etc. etc., just like Peking. Close to Mukden are the ancestral graves of the Manchu dynasty.

THE GATE OF VICTORY,

MUKDEN.

## THE WEST GATE OF KIALING FU.

A MOST picturesque entrance to the city. These gates are closed at sunset and opened at sunrise, the gongs and other instruments notifying the hours of opening and closing.

THE WEST GATE OF KIALING FU.

## THE WEST GATE OF HANGCHOW.

One of the friendliest cities to the foreigner. The cry of "Foreign devil!" is never heard within its walls. The people have had time to learn how much they profit by the trade the foreigner brings, and by the efforts of the missionaries to ameliorate the condition of the very poor by their hospitals. Hangchow is a great centre of the silk trade. The whole city, which has a population of 700,000, and the principal street of which is five miles long, is surrounded by a wall faced with hewn stone, such as is shown in the photograph. It is pierced by many gates. It is a treaty port, two days' journey from the great foreign settlement of Shanghai.

THE WEST GATE OF HANGCHOW.

# THE GATE OF A FORBIDDEN CITY.

In contrast to Hangchow, though only two miles from a treaty port, it is believed that no foreigner has ever had the foolhardiness to enter this gate. It is a city of the fifth order only; but such is the hatred and detestation in which the foreigner is held, it would be almost certain death to him to enter it. This hatred of the foreigner is a very curious characteristic of the country. No one can tell how it has arisen, for though one can understand that the attempts of Western nations to force open the ports of the country, and the seizure of territory by certain of them, and perhaps the advent of the missionaries, are causes enough to provoke opposition and hatred, they do not account for its ferocity. The idea of the Chinaman and the Chinawoman is that the foreigner is a child-eater, that no children are safe within his reach, that he kills children that he may take their eyes and hearts to make into his medicines. This belief is so deeply rooted, that when the cry of "Foreigner!" is raised, in almost any city, the women will run into the streets, snatch up their children, and carry them for safety into their homes; and the cry raised is always "Foreign devil!" "Child-eater!" It may be noted that a similar suspicion exists over a great part of Central and Southern Europe towards the Jews, who are charged with murdering children to mingle their blood with sacrifices.

CHINESE PICTURES

THE GATE OF A FORBIDDEN CITY.

## SILK REELING.

Hangchow is the city of silk, a wealthy and generally well-to-do city. Everything speaks to the visitor of silk. The country is covered by the mulberry tree, which grows in every available spot. There are thousands of hand-looms. In the picture given, the silk is being wound into a thread from the cocoons, which are thrown into a pan of hot water, kept hot by a small furnace; the ends of the threads are disentangled from the cocoon, four or five of them taken together are given a twist by the right hand, whilst the left winds the thread on to the wheel. This is the first step in, and the foundation of, all silk manufacture.

SILK REELING.

## A TYPICAL ENTRANCE TO A HOUSE.

This particular house was at Mukden, in Manchuria. The main building is surrounded by a courtyard. The outer building contains the servants' rooms. They live around the courtyard, the family occupying the central building. The windows of the servants' rooms may be seen in the outer wall. The pillars of woodwork are highly decorated, and in the courtyard itself there is always a flower-garden. Comparing this simple house with a palace such as the English Legation, it will be seen that the latter is but an amplification of the ordinary house, the number of courtyards surrounding the chief dwelling being greater, but the principle of construction being the same.

A TYPICAL ENTRANCE TO A HOUSE.

## THE GUEST HALL IN A CHINESE HOUSE, WAN HSIEN, SZE CHUAN.

Every good house has its guest hall, and every invited guest knows his place in it. A Chinaman is wretched in a foreign house because he does not know his place in it. Etiquette prescribes everything in China, and no matter who or what the visitor may be, he knows which chair to take. No matter who may be present, he is never disturbed or distressed; and when tea or pipes are introduced he enjoys them as though he were in his own house, and both host and visitor are perfectly at their ease.

THE GUEST HALL IN A CHINESE HOUSE,
WAN HSIEN, SZE CHUAN.

## A CHINESE VILLAGE.

On the Min or Fu River, above the point where it rims into the Upper Yangtze. The black-and-white architecture of the villages reminds one constantly of Switzerland and the Tyrol. As to the village, it is by no means lacking in organisation. Every village consists of a group or groups of families with their head men, and over the head men are the district magistrates. The family is the centre of everything. The members are bound together by the strongest ties, and the family is responsible for the individual. The people have quite a genius for self-government, and every village is self-governing, having its privileges, which no one dare interfere with.

CHINESE PICTURES

A CHINESE VILLAGE.

## A FARMHOUSE IN THE HAKKA COUNTRY, SOUTHERN CHINA.

An illustration of the Patriarchal system. When a son marries and brings home his wife, he literally brings her home—that is, to his father's house; but a new gable is added to those in existence, and the house increased for the accommodation of the new family, a custom which has its counterpart in Italy and other parts of Europe to-day.

A FARMHOUSE IN THE HAKKA COUNTRY,
SOUTHERN CHINA.

## A MARKET PLACE OR MARKET STREET IN SZE CHUAN.

All through the Empire province of Sze Chuan, the western province of the Yangtze Basin, markets are held in the market street, specially reserved for the purpose. On market days the street is crowded by thousands of people, the tea and other shops are overflowing, and the noise and shouts of the bargainers are deafening. The shops are generally owned by farmers in the neighbourhood, who let them for the use of merchants on market day. On other than market days they are like deserted villages. No one is to be seen but the caretaker and his family, who are shown in the photograph with the inevitable dog and pig and buffalo. The building on the right is a temple.

A MARKET PLACE OR MARKET STREET
IN SZE CHUAN.

## THE COBBLER.

A very important personage in China. He deals, however, with men's shoes only. The women wear tiny satin or brocaded things which they mostly make and mend themselves. They are from two to three inches long, and with hard-working women in the fields the feet never extend four inches. The Chinese practice of binding the feet of girls is very old. It is, of course, only a fashion, but it has the sanction of great antiquity. A girl with her feet the normal shape would stand no chance of getting married. The binding process begins very early—between four and five generally, though sometimes it is postponed to a later date, when the process is much more painful. The four toes are doubled under the foot, and the large toe folded on the top. When bound together a sort of club-foot or hoof results, but the women manage to walk in spite of their deformity. To a western eye, the movement resembles a waddle rather than a walk.

THE COBBLER.

## CARRYING LIQUID MANURE TO THE FIELDS.

In the great fertile plain of Sze Chuan, where four crops a year are taken off the ground, this is an enormous industry. The Chinese cannot afford any waste; everything must go back to the ground. We seek to get over the deterioration of the land by changing the crops. In China the same crops have been grown on the land for a thousand years, and it shows no signs of deterioration.

CARRYING LIQUID MANURE

TO THE FIELDS.

## THE MARRIAGE CHAIR.

In which a bride of the upper classes is carried to her husband's home. It is often a very beautiful thing, gorgeous with its embroidery in silk and colours. People who are not rich enough to have one of their own can hire them for the occasion. In China large families are the rule. If a mother dies, the women of the village suckle and bring up the child between them, and children are not weaned until they are from three to five years of age. Chinese women are very modest and kind-hearted, are faithful wives, and, according to their own notions, good mothers. In Sze Chuan there is no trace of infanticide, but it is practised in many parts of the Empire.

THE MARRIAGE CHAIR.

# MODE OF CARRYING CASH AND BABIES.

In travelling, the carriage of money is a great annoyance, owing to the smallness of its value and the large number of coins or "cash" necessary to make up an amount of any size. Exchanging eighteen shillings English for brass cash, the weight of them amounted to seventy-two pounds, which had to be carried by the coolies. These cash have a square hole in the middle, and are strung together upon a piece of straw twist. Should the straw break, the loss of time in getting up the pieces is much more than the loss of the money. The Chinese are honest, very keen at a bargain, but when the bargain is made the Chinaman may be depended on to keep it.

MODE OF CARRYING CASH AND BABIES.

# A PAI-FANG, OR WIDOWS ARCH.

These are often very fine structures in stone, wonderfully carved, or in wood highly decorated. It is not uncommon to enter a town under quite a succession of them. Very fine ones are often found at the entrance of very squalid villages. They are erections put up to honour widows who, faithful to the memory of their husbands, have remained widows, devoting themselves to good works and to the service of their parents-in-law, which is the great duty of every good wife. Permission of the Emperor has to be obtained for their erection. The various towns and villages take pride in their "widows' arches." It is not uncommon to find a shrine for the burning of incense beside the arch.

A PAI-FANG, OR WIDOWS ARCH.

## TWO SOLDIERS OF SZE CHUAN.

The military are usually dressed in picturesque but unserviceable, not to say grotesque costumes, the carnation red, beloved of the Chinese, and blue being the prevailing colours. They carry fans, and often paper umbrellas. They are ill-trained and indolent, lounging about the gates of the cities or the streets gambling and smoking. Their curse is that they have nothing to do.

TWO SOLDIERS OF SZE CHUAN.

## OPIUM CULTURE ENCROACHING ON THE RICE LANDS, SZE CHUAN.

The great system of irrigation at Sze Chuan was intended for the cultivation of rice only; but the great and terrible growth in the demand for opium has caused the cultivation of the poppy so to increase that it is encroaching on the rice lands.

This may be regarded as the saddest and most terrible fact as regards the future of China.

The use of opium is of comparatively recent date, but the growth and spreading of the habit has been most rapid. At the first, both local and government officials did their best to stop it and to stamp out the culture of the poppy; but although laws were passed making death the penalty for its cultivation they became a dead letter, until to-day it is estimated that eighty per cent. of the men and fifty per cent. of the women, in one or two populous provinces, are opium smokers. They do not all smoke to excess. There are moderate smokers as we have our moderate drinkers; but all through the province of Sze Chuan the opium shops are as thick as the gin shops in the lower parts of London.

It is not necessary to dilate on the effects of opium when freely indulged in. They are too well known. China's only hope is to emancipate herself from the vice that is eating away her manhood. But will she be able to do it?

OPIUM CULTURE ENCROACHING
ON THE RICE LANDS, SZE CHUAN.

# About The Author

**Isabella Lucy Bird** was born in 1831, and was one of the most well-traveled and intrepid of English explorers in the 19th century. She wrote books about her journeys through many regions, including Japan, Korea, Hawaii, China and the American Rockies. She died in 1904.